Technology All Around Us

Medicine

Dr. K. R. Routh

A^+
Smart Apple Media

First published in 2005 by Franklin Watts
96 Leonard Street, London EC2A 4XD

Franklin Watts Australia
Level 17/207 Kent Street, Sydney NSW 2000

Produced by Arcturus Publishing Ltd.
26/27 Bickels Yard, 151–153 Bermondsey Street, London SE1 3HA

Series concept: Alex Woolf, Editor: Alex Woolf, Designer: Simon
Borrough, Picture researcher: Glass Onion Pictures

Picture Credits:
Science Photo Library: 4 (Richard T. Nowitz), 5 (Simon Fraser), 6 (Mark
Thomas), 7 (Alfred Pasieka), 8 (Saturn Stills), 9 (Zephyr), 10 (John Greim),
11 (David M. Martin, M.D.), 12 (Antonia Reeve), 13 (Antonia Reeve), 14
(Chris Priest), 15 (John Bavosi), 16 (Catherine Ursillo), 17 (James King-
Holmes), 18 (Du Cane Medical Imaging Ltd), 19 (Ouellette & Theroux,
Publiphoto Diffusion), 21 (Hank Morgan), 22 (Deep Light Productions), 24
(Siu), 25 (Antonia Reeve), 26 (Horacio Sormani), 27 (David Nunuk), 28 and
cover (NIH/Custom Medical Stock Photo), 29 (John Bavosi).
Topham Picturepoint: 23 (Richard Ellis/The Image Works).

Published in the United States by Smart Apple Media
2140 Howard Drive West, North Mankato, Minnesota 56003

Library of Congress Cataloging-in-Publication Data

Routh, Kristina, 1961–
Medicine / by K. R. Routh.
p. cm. — (Technology all around us)
ISBN 1-58340-751-0
1. Medical technology—Juvenile literature. 2. Medicine—Juvenile literature.
I. Title. II. Series.

R855.4.R686 2005
610'.28—dc22   2004059015

9 8 7 6 5 4 3 2 1

Contents

Machines and Medicine

Technology plays a very important role in medicine. Machines are used every day to find out what's wrong when someone is sick, to do the work of worn-out or damaged body parts, and even to keep people alive.

Seeing Into the Body

Machines can look inside the body without having to cut the skin. X-ray machines, ultrasound, and medical scanners take pictures of our bones, internal organs, and blood vessels.

Tiny cameras on long tubes or in capsules can go inside the body to look for problems in the intestines and other body parts. This kind of technology helps doctors determine what is wrong and decide what treatment is needed.

>> Looking Forward

Digital Doctors Complex computer programs are being written that can help determine what is wrong with a patient. The patient answers questions asked by the computer, which then makes a likely diagnosis.

One day, these computers may be able to diagnose illnesses on their own, but most patients will probably still want to see a human doctor when they are sick.

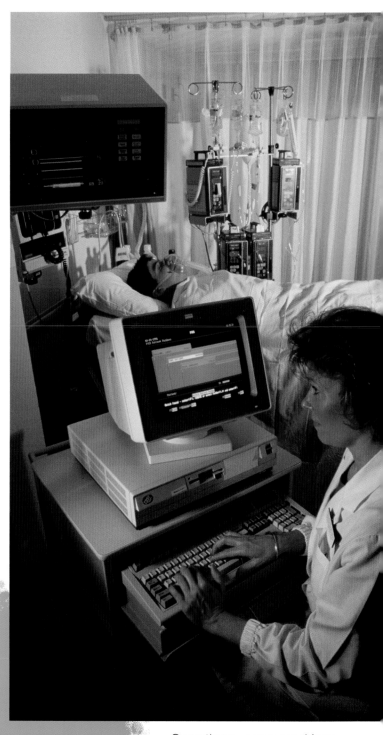

Sometimes, many machines are needed to help look after patients in an intensive care ward.

Helping the Body Work

From hearing aids to artificial legs, technology can be used to assist or replace many different functions of the body.

Artificial hearts boost the strength of a failing human heart, and dialysis machines do the work of damaged kidneys. Without these man-made organs, many people would lead a more difficult and uncertain life.

Some technology provides "life support"—without it, a person would die. Ventilators and heart-lung machines perform the vital roles of breathing and pumping blood. Often, tiny babies born too early are kept alive in high-tech incubators that monitor their every move.

Humans Still Needed

Technology is important in modern medicine, but it will never replace the skills and care of our healthcare workers. Machines cannot offer the human contact we need when we are very sick.

Although stethoscopes have been around for nearly 200 years, they are still used every day by doctors and nurses around the world.

Looking Back

The Stethoscope Doctors and nurses have been using special medical tools for many years. The stethoscope has been used to listen to the heart and lungs since its invention in 1816 by French doctor Rene Laennec.

Although there are newer, more complicated ways to do this, the stethoscope is still used by doctors in hospitals all over the world.

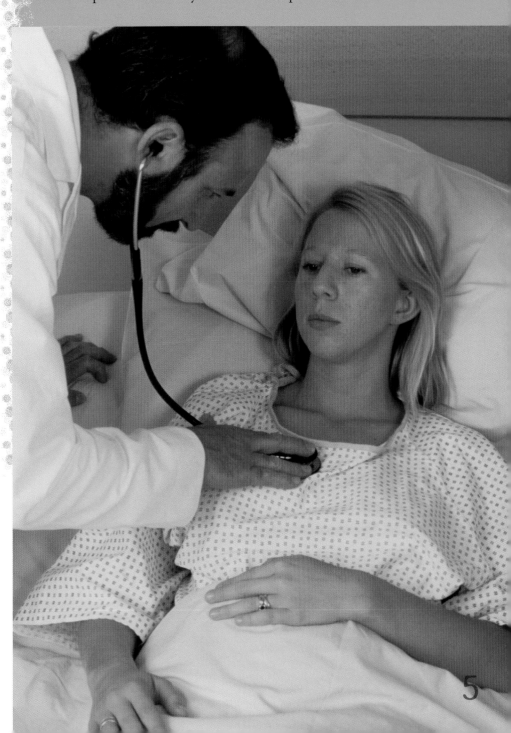

When a person becomes sick, doctors use X-ray machines and body scanners to "look" inside the body to see what the problem is.

Looking Back

X-ray Pictures X rays were discovered in 1895 by German physicist Wilhelm Roentgen. He took an X-ray picture of his wife's hand, and newspapers around the world reported the news of his find.

Doctors soon realized how useful these new pictures could be for finding broken bones and even lost bullets.

The doughnut-shaped **CAT** scanner uses computers to take pictures of the inside of the patient's body.

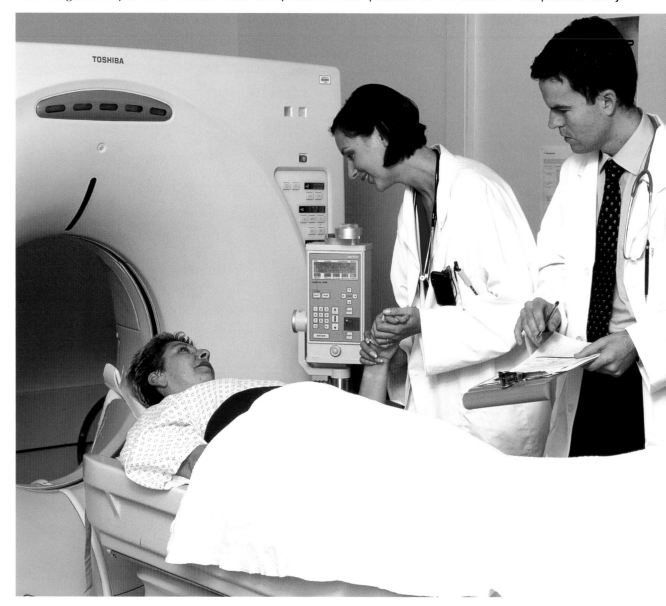

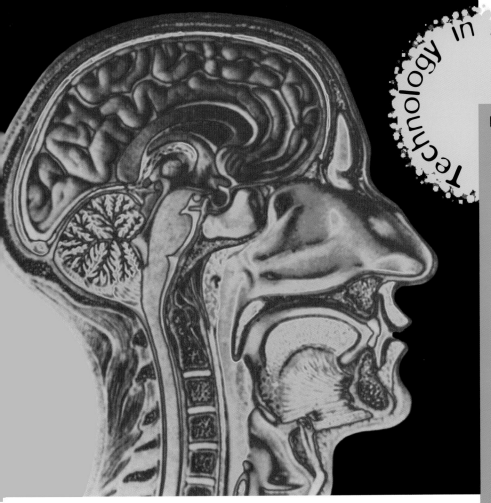

Scans, such as this MRI (Magnetic Resonance Imaging) scan of a healthy head, can show great detail from inside the body.

Brain Scan

Little Sara was just 17 months old when her mother became worried that she was not holding her head up properly. Doctors recommended that she have a special test called an MRI scan done to look inside her head.

The doctors were surprised to find a tumor (lump) inside that was pressing against her brain. She needed an operation to remove it. Luckily, it wasn't the kind of tumor that is very harmful and grows back, so the doctors think she will be fine.

X-ray Machines

An X-ray machine is similar to a camera. But unlike normal photographs, X-ray pictures show the inside of the body.

When an X-ray picture is held up to a strong light, bones appear white, and air-filled spaces (such as the lungs) appear black. Soft tissues such as the heart and intestines appear gray.

X-ray pictures are useful for finding broken bones and for looking for diseases such as cancer or infection. And if a person accidentally swallows a solid object, an X ray can be used to find out where it has gone.

Body Scanners

Sometimes doctors need to see inside the body in great detail. This is when a body scanner—a large, complicated machine that uses fast computers—may be used. The pictures it produces look like slices of the body and show internal parts very clearly. You may have heard of one type—the CAT scanner. (CAT stands for Computerized Axial Tomography.)

The patient being scanned lies on a bed that moves inside the doughnut-shaped scanner. It is a bit noisy, but it doesn't hurt.

Body scanners can show if there is disease or damage in any part of the body. These scans cost a lot of money (much more than most X rays), so they are used only when absolutely necessary.

Seeing with Sound

Bats and dolphins use sound waves to find out what is around them. We can use sound in a similar way to "see" inside the body. This method of looking inside the body is called ultrasound scanning. It is very safe and widely used.

The ultrasound machine has a part called a probe that looks like a microphone. Placed against the skin, it sends sound waves into the part of the body being examined. The waves bounce back to form a picture that appears on a monitor. The monitor shows a moving image, like a video, from which snapshots can be taken.

Looking Forward

Virtual Reality In the future, surgeons may be able to operate inside the body by using computer-generated "virtual" images provided by ultrasound. The surgeon will wear a headset and will see himself performing the operation as though he is playing a video or computer game.

Seeing Unborn Babies

Ultrasound is used to find out whether a baby is growing well inside its mother. Most pregnant women have at least one ultrasound scan. It is safe for the baby and the mother. The tiny, growing baby can be seen many months before it is born. Its heart and other body parts can be checked and measured. Sometimes doctors can even tell if it is a boy or a girl.

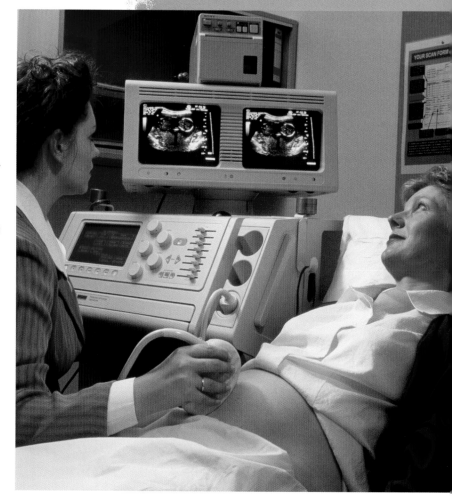

This pregnant woman is having an ultrasound scan. Her unborn baby can be seen on the monitors.

Watching Blood Moving

This ultrasound scan shows blood slowing down because of a blocked artery (slow-moving blood shows up green; faster blood shows up red).

Ultrasound is also used to study the way blood flows through the heart and around the body. If an artery is blocked by a blood clot, the blood will stop flowing through it. An ultrasound scan can show this and help the surgeon decide whether an operation is needed to clear the artery.

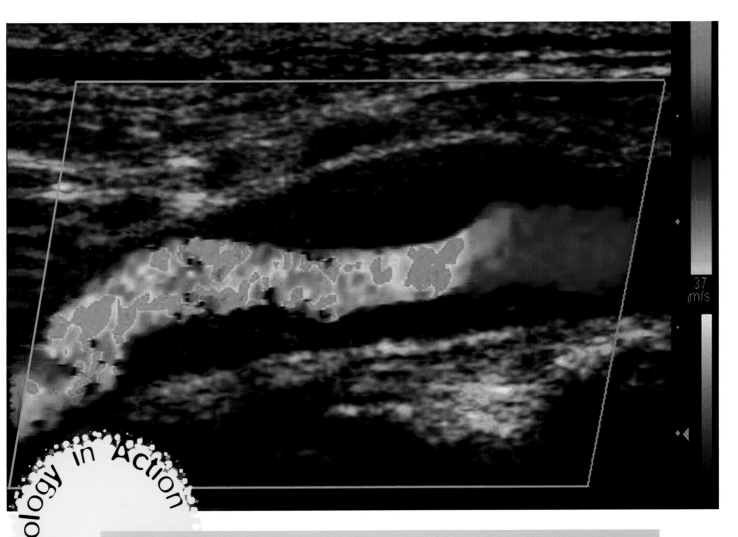

37 m/s

Technology in Action

Ultrasound Test

It's January 2001, and Jenny Moss is having a test called an echocardiogram. This test uses ultrasound to look closely at her heart and the way blood flows through it.

Jenny is having the test done because her doctor heard a murmur (an abnormal heart sound) when he listened to her chest. He was worried that she might have a damaged heart. Fortunately, the test shows that everything is fine.

If you want to take a picture of the inside of your mouth, you could do it with an ordinary camera. But imagine that you need a picture of the region farther down, inside your stomach. You would need a very tiny camera, and it would need to be attached to the end of a long, flexible tube.

Doctors use an endoscope to look down inside a patient's nose. The endoscope sends pictures to the monitor behind them.

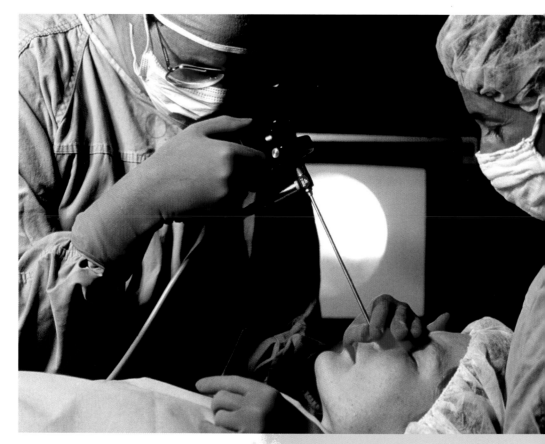

Endoscopes

Cameras like this, called endoscopes, are used in medicine in many ways. Some go down through the mouth into the throat, stomach, or lungs.

Some go up through a person's bottom to look at the intestines. And some are used during operations, pushed through tiny cuts in the skin while the patient is asleep.

Doctors look at the pictures sent back by the endoscopes to see if there are any areas of disease or damage. Sometimes they use a tiny tool in the endoscope to take a sample of tissue to look at more closely under a microscope.

Looking Back

Limited Vision Before the invention of endoscopes, doctors examining a sick patient could see into the body only a short way. They couldn't look around corners. For example, a doctor could look into the mouth to see a sore throat but could not look farther down into the stomach to see an ulcer.

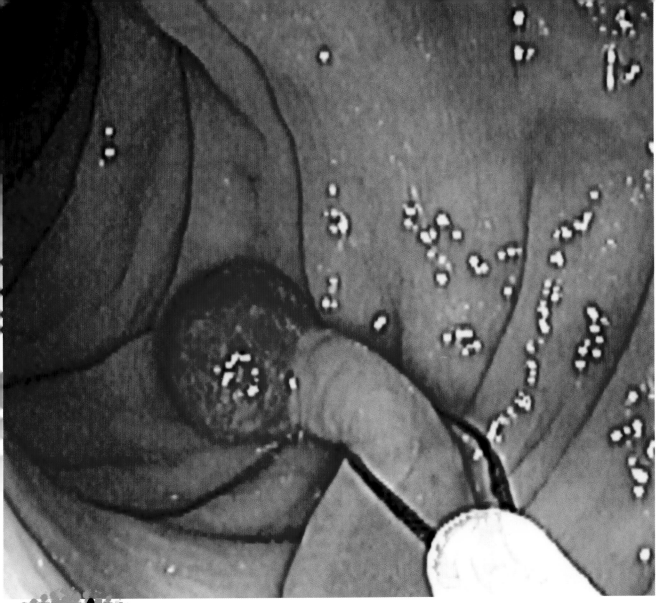

This picture from an endoscope shows a small growth, called a polyp, being removed from inside the intestine using a loop of sharp wire.

View from the Inside

Samuel, age 65, has been having strange stomach aches and diarrhea for many years. His doctor decides to use the new capsule camera to try to find the problem.

Sam finds the test simple and painless. The pictures taken by the camera show that he has a disease of the intestine called Crohn's disease. Now he is receiving the right treatment and is doing well.

The Camera Pill

Endoscopes have a problem: they aren't long enough or flexible enough to go all the way down inside the intestines. So scientists invented the capsule camera—a camera in the form of a large pill.

The patient swallows the "pill," and it takes pictures as it goes through the hard-to-reach parts of the intestines and out the other end.

In the past, when surgeons wanted to perform an operation, they would have to make a large cut in the skin to be able to see and work inside the body. These long cuts—perhaps two to four inches (5–10 cm) or more in length—were then stitched up and took several weeks to heal.

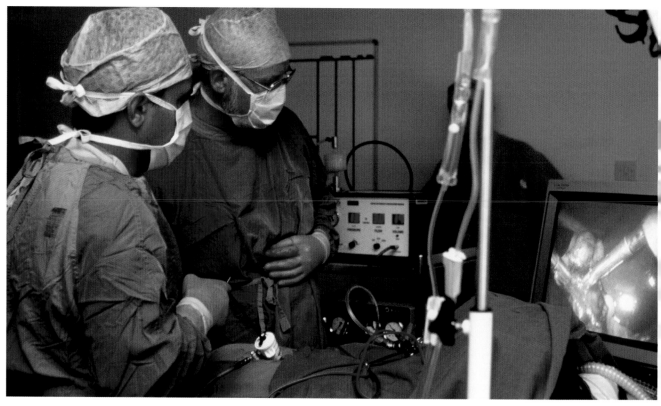

Surgeons use instruments on long tubes to operate inside a patient's stomach. They look at the monitor to see what is happening inside as they work.

Today, many operations can be performed through tiny cuts perhaps one or two centimeters long. This is known as keyhole surgery. In these operations, the surgeon usually makes several small cuts just large enough to allow the special surgical instruments through.

Keyhole surgery is changing the way hospitals and surgeons work. Smaller surgical wounds mean that patients recover more quickly and are less likely to get an infection. Their hospital stay is usually shorter; many go home the same day.

Looking Forward

Remote Control It is likely that an increasing number of operations will be done by keyhole surgery in the future.

Medical scientists are working on ways to perform these operations by remote control, as many of the tiny instruments used are difficult to work with using the human hand.

Surgical Instruments

A surgeon uses several different types of instruments to perform keyhole surgery. To see what is going on inside the body, he uses an endoscope, a tube with a camera at the end (see pages 10–11).

Then, depending on the type of operation, he uses other tiny instruments that cut tissue, hold internal organs, or clip blood vessels. Each of these instruments is at the end of a long tube that is pushed through a small cut in the skin.

Special, long-handled instruments are used in keyhole surgery.

Technology in Action

Quick Recovery
In January 2002, a 40-year-old woman named Emma Westwood went to her local hospital. She was there to have an operation called a cholecystectomy, in which her gallbladder would be removed by keyhole surgery. If she had had the operation 10 years earlier, she would have had a large cut and would have been in the hospital for 10 days. Emma felt fine after the operation and left the hospital the same day. She was back at work four weeks later.

Most of us take our ears for granted, but some people need the help of technology to hear.

Hearing Aids

Many people who are hard-of-hearing use hearing aids. A hearing aid is a battery-operated electronic device that receives sound through a microphone. It then amplifies the sound (makes it louder) and sends it to the ear through a tiny speaker.

Hearing aids work only if the person can still hear sounds. They will not help someone who is completely deaf.

There are several different kinds of hearing aids. In one of the most common types, the main part of the device tucks behind the ear, and a plastic part extends down into the entrance of the ear.

Looking Back

Ear Trumpets Invented in the 1800s, the first hearing aids were known as ear trumpets. They were made of various materials, including silver and tortoiseshell.

These aids were not electronic devices. They were just like large funnels that people spoke into so that the user could hear what was being said.

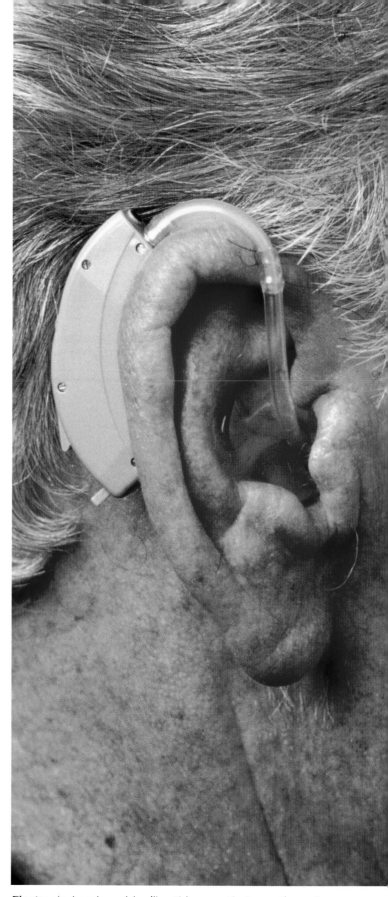

Electronic hearing aids, like this one that mostly rests behind the ear, are made up of a microphone, an amplifier, and a tiny speaker.

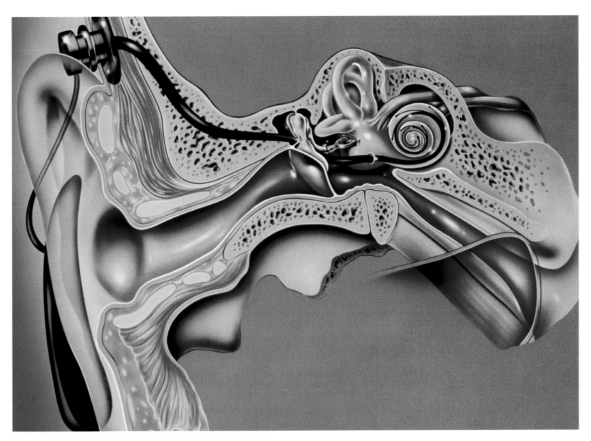

This cutaway picture shows how a cochlear implant fits inside the ear.

Cochlear Implants

If someone is deaf or extremely hard-of-hearing, he or she may be given a different electronic device called a cochlear implant. This device is named after the cochlea, the part of the inner ear that turns sound waves into nerve signals to be sent to the brain.

A cochlear implant is a tiny machine that helps to do the job of a real cochlea when that part of the ear is not working properly. The device has some parts that are implanted under the skin behind the ear in a surgical operation, and some parts that are worn on a belt or in a pocket.

Technology in Action

New Sounds

Jake, age 15, had worn hearing aids for many years but had always been able to hear a little. Then, one day, he found he couldn't hear anything at all. His doctors suggested that a cochlear implant might help, and the operation was performed in January 2004.

At first, Jake didn't like it. Everything sounded too different. But he soon got used to the implant, and now his parents say he is "like a new kid."

Artificial limbs can allow people to live normal lives—and even to play sports.

Technology in Action

Fighting Back

When American athlete John Register lost his lower left leg in an accident during training in 1994, it looked like his career in track was over. But John was determined to compete again.

With the help of a specially designed artificial leg, he soon began training in sprints and the long jump. He went on to win the silver medal in the long jump in the Sydney 2000 Paralympics.

Imagine what it would be like to be without an arm or a leg. People can lose limbs through accidents, cancer, or war injuries. Some children are born without a limb, or with one that has not grown properly.

No man-made limb can ever be as good as the real thing. But modern artificial arms and legs can help give their users an almost normal lifestyle.

Artificial limbs—also called limb prostheses—are made from a mixture of materials, including plastic, metal, and foam rubber. New, lightweight materials such as Kevlar, carbon fiber, and titanium are helping to make artificial limbs stronger and lighter. Where there is a joint—for instance, at the elbow or the knee—artificial limbs are designed to bend the same way as the real joint.

Movement of an artificial limb can be "mechanical," in which the person's own muscle power moves it through a series of cables. Or, movement can be "electronic," in which the power comes from a battery. Sometimes both methods are used.

Special Features

There are many types of artificial limbs, with some designed for certain activities. For example, there are sports limbs with special features that allow the person to run faster or to throw and catch a ball. There are even "swimming" legs that have holes to allow water to fill them so that they don't float too much.

Looking Forward

Thought Power Some scientists believe that one day there will be artificial limbs that work by thought alone. Special sensors will be connected to the brain that can send messages directly to the man-made limb.

This is very similar to the way our nerves work and would be a great breakthrough in making these limbs as real as possible.

An artificial hand has to be very complex to perform the job of a real hand well.

The heart is a large muscle that beats around 70 times per minute every day of our lives. There is a special section of heart muscle called a pacemaker that tells the rest of the muscle how often to contract.

Mechanical Pacemakers

If the heart's own pacemaker doesn't work properly, a mechanical pacemaker might be used. This is a small, battery-operated electronic device that is implanted under the skin in a patient's chest. It has wires that connect to the heart to check how often the heart is beating.

If the heart beats too slowly, the pacemaker sends an electrical signal through the wires that makes the heart muscle contract.

This colored X ray shows a surgically implanted pacemaker.

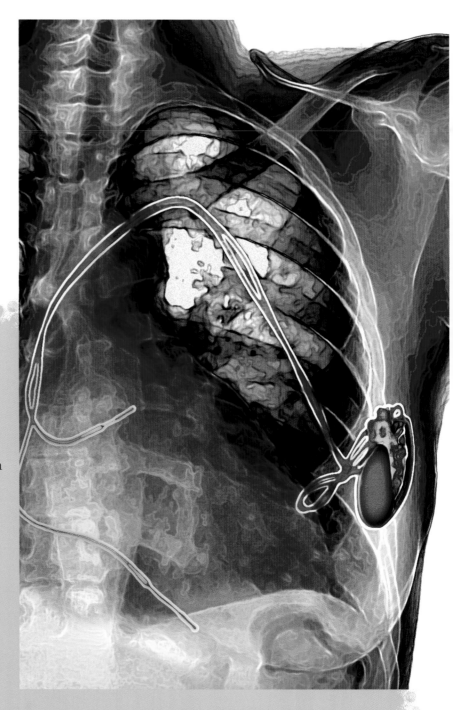

Looking Back

The First Pacemaker The first mechanical pacemaker was invented in 1950, but it wasn't until 1958 that a team of Swedish doctors implanted one inside a human body. The patient died after three hours.

The next year, American doctor Wilson Greatbach was more successful. The pacemaker he developed kept one of his patients alive for 18 months.

Defibrillators

You have probably seen a defibrillator used in medical dramas on TV. The doctor holds a "paddle" in each hand, shouts "clear," and then presses the paddles to the patient's chest and gives an electric shock.

A defibrillator is used when a person's heart muscle starts to quiver, or fibrillate, instead of contracting properly. No blood gets pumped, and the person will die unless a proper heartbeat can be started.

The paddles send an electrical impulse through the heart that makes the heart muscle contract properly. The doctor has everyone stand back so they won't get a jolt of electricity, too.

A monitor shows the heart's electrical activity so the doctor can see how well the heart has responded.

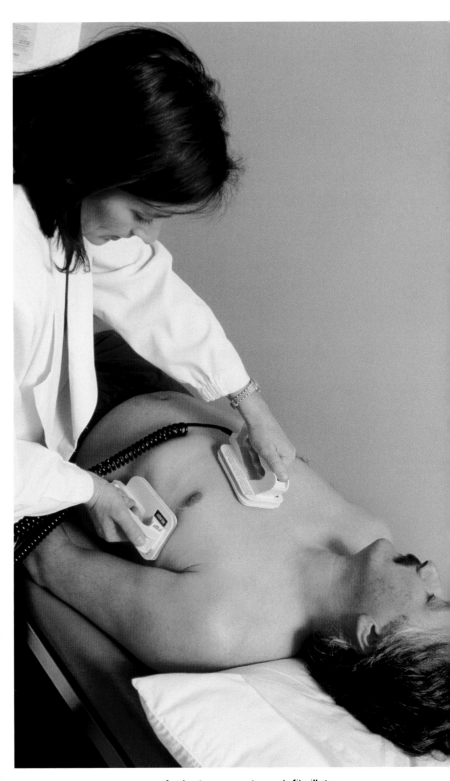

A doctor uses two defibrillator paddles, sending an electric shock to make the heart beat properly again.

 **Looking Forward**

On-the-Spot Treatment New "semi-automatic" defibrillators are designed to offer step-by-step instructions to the person using them. Ambulance personnel, firefighters, and police officers are among the people who can be trained to use these machines.

In the future, these defibrillators may be available in public places so that people who need this life-saving treatment can be helped immediately.

19

Sometimes, because of disease, the heart becomes too weak to do its job properly. A heart transplant is then needed. A donor heart is taken from someone who has recently died.

Sadly, there are never enough donor hearts, so medical scientists have developed machines that can do the work of the heart, at least for a while.

Helping the Heart

Sometimes a heart can still pump but needs some extra help. Left ventricular assist devices (LVADs) are machines that work together with a person's own heart.

In the past, LVADs were large machines used only in hospitals. Newer, smaller models are now available that can be put inside the body so the person can walk around and live fairly normally.

One type is the Jarvik 2000, which is like a tiny, battery-operated engine. It is put inside the heart and helps to push the blood through. The batteries are usually recharged through a socket in the skin behind the ear.

Looking Forward

From Living Tissue Mechanical devices that help or replace the heart are improving, but many people think there is a better option—hearts made from living tissue grown in laboratories.

This may seem like science fiction, but it could happen one day. And these living hearts could have far fewer problems than their mechanical cousins.

Dr. Robert Jarvik (left), inventor of the Jarvik 2000, holds his invention near the chest of Peter Houghton, the first patient to receive the LVAD in June 2000.

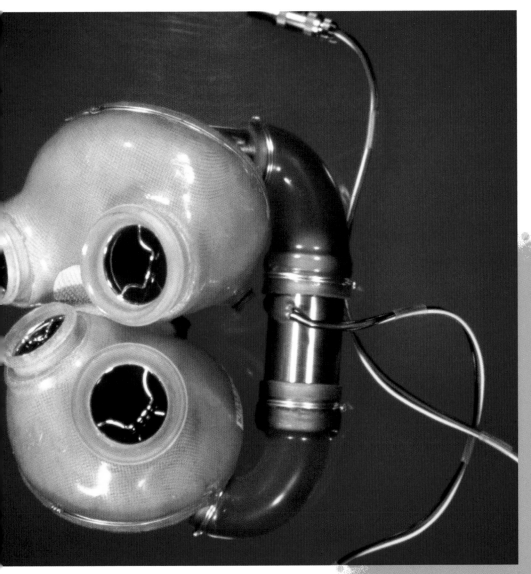

The Jarvik 7, an artificial heart made of aluminium and plastic, was used in the first human implant in 1982.

Replacing a Heart

Replacing the heart completely has been less successful. For many years, scientists have been trying to make an artificial heart that is safe and works well.

One of the biggest problems is that man-made materials tend to make the blood form clots (solid lumps), which can block important blood vessels.

One artificial heart being developed in the U.S. is known as the Abiocor. One day, this type of heart may help many people who would otherwise die of heart failure.

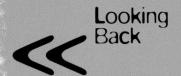

Looking Back

Artificial Hearts The earliest artificial hearts were tested in animals in the 1950s. In 1969, the Texas Heart Institute successfully kept a patient alive for 60 hours with their model.

And in 1982, in Utah, a patient named Barney Clark was given an artificial heart (the Jarvik 7) that kept him alive for 112 days.

To stay alive, the human body needs to take in oxygen and send it around to all of its parts through the bloodstream. Normally, the lungs and heart do this, but sometimes the body needs the help of machines.

Breathing Machines

Sometimes people are not able to breathe on their own. This may be due to an accident or because they are rendered unconscious for a surgical operation. Machines called ventilators can help them breathe.

A ventilator pushes a mixture of air and pure oxygen through a tube into the person's lungs. This is done in regular "breaths" several times a minute.

Ventilators have many different monitors and alarms that alert doctors or nurses if something is wrong with the patient or the machine. This is critical, because the patient needs the machine to stay alive.

Bypassing the Heart and Lungs

A surgeon may need to operate on the heart, and this cannot be done if the heart muscle is moving. So, a cardiopulmonary bypass, or heart-lung machine, is used.

This machine has long tubes that collect blood as it arrives at the heart. The blood is then sent through the heart-lung machine, which loads it with oxygen and then pumps it back into the main artery of the body, the aorta.

Because the machine does the pumping, the heart muscle can be made to stop beating for the operation.

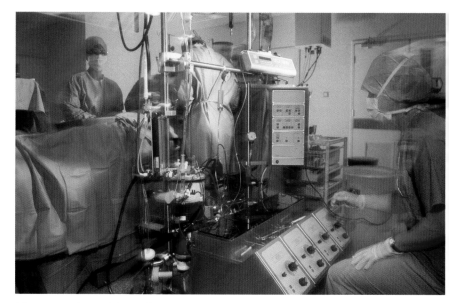

The complicated heart-lung machine does the work of the heart while doctors perform a heart operation.

Looking Back

Iron Lungs Before a vaccine was discovered in 1955, a viral disease called polio affected millions of people, leaving many unable to breathe on their own. These people had to spend weeks or months living in large, coffin-shaped ventilator machines called iron lungs. Photographs from the time show entire wards of these iron lungs in action.

Telling the Body to Breathe

Christopher Reeve, who starred in the movie *Superman*, was paralyzed in a horseback riding accident in 1995. He needed a mechanical ventilator to breathe. His portable machine weighed around 44 pounds (20 kg). It was smaller than a hospital ventilator and let him live in his own home.

In 2003, Reeve had surgery to implant a new electronic device into his chest. This device told the diaphragm (the main breathing muscle) to contract. Sadly, Reeve died in 2004.

Actor Christopher Reeve needed a machine to help him breathe after being injured in a horseback riding accident.

It is very important that the right amount of water is kept inside the body and that the blood has the correct balance of chemicals. This is mainly the job of the kidneys, which get rid of unwanted water and chemicals by making urine.

When the kidneys are not working properly, a person is said to be in renal (or kidney) failure.

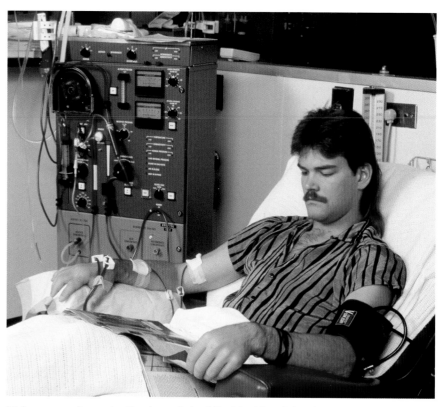

This man relaxes in the hospital while his blood is cleaned by a dialysis machine. This can take several hours.

Dialysis Machines

People in renal failure need the help of medical technology to keep them alive. In most cases, this means they have to use an artificial kidney called a dialysis machine.

Dialysis machines may be used for patients who are staying in the hospital, or they may be used in special clinics by visiting patients.

During dialysis, a tube is put into a vein in the patient's arm, and blood travels through the tube into the machine. Inside the machine, the blood comes into contact with a very thin sheet, or membrane, that separates it from another liquid.

Waste chemicals from the blood pass through the membrane into the liquid, which is eventually thrown away. The cleaned blood is returned to the body through another thin tube.

Looking Back

The First Artificial Kidney Sadly, before dialysis machines were invented, people with kidney failure would die as waste substances built up in their blood.

The first artificial kidney was made in 1943 by Willem J. Kolff, a Dutch doctor who later worked in the U.S. Many people are now kept alive by modern versions of this machine.

>> Looking Forward

More Transplants One day, it may be possible to make artificial kidneys that can be implanted in the body. It would be better, however, to make more kidneys available for transplant. Campaigners are working hard to tell people about the importance of carrying organ donor cards, saying that the carrier would like to donate his or her kidneys in the event of a sudden death.

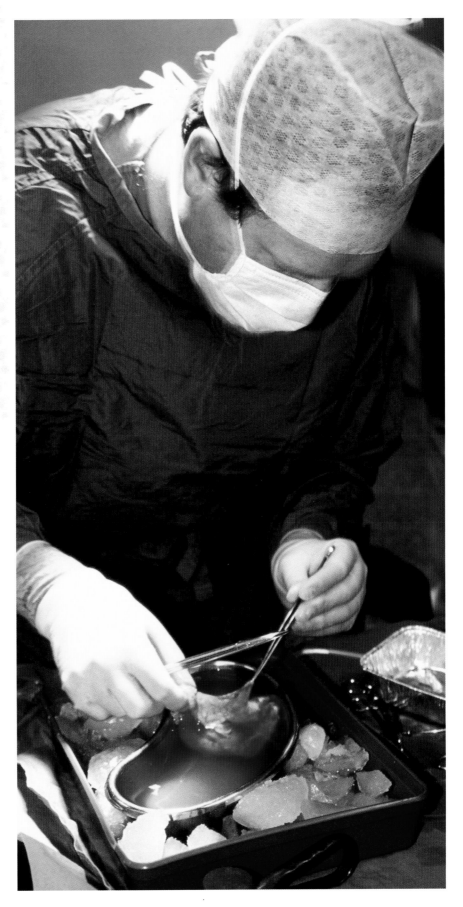

A surgeon prepares a donor kidney before implanting it into someone with kidney failure.

This blood-cleaning process is carried out again and again for up to five hours, three times a week.

For some people, dialysis is needed only for a short time, then the kidneys recover. Others may get a new donor kidney, which means they no longer need dialysis. Many people, however, must use a dialysis machine for the rest of their lives.

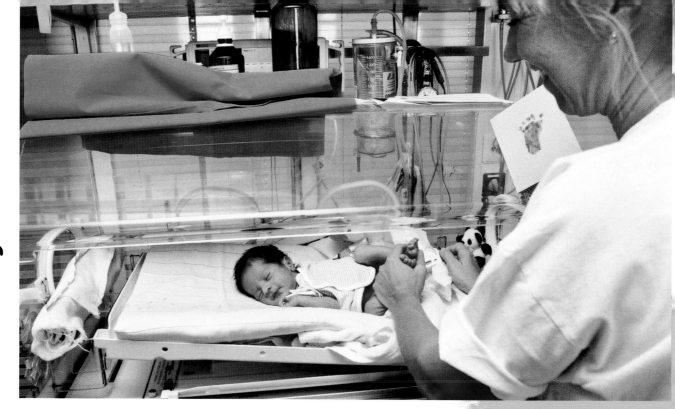

This tiny baby is being carefully looked after in a special cot called an incubator.

Some babies need special care after they are born, especially those who are born too early—known as premature babies. These babies may be very small and have problems with breathing and staying warm. They are also more likely to get an infection.

Incubators

Premature babies (as well as some that are born with medical problems) may need to be looked after in an incubator for a while. An incubator is a special box-like crib that has a heater to keep the baby warm.

Some incubators have a see-through lid that helps to keep heat and moisture in. The lid usually has hand-sized holes so that nurses can reach the baby without opening the lid.

While the baby is inside the incubator, its breathing, temperature, and heartbeat are closely watched. Several kinds of wires and pads are gently attached to the baby to carry information to electronic monitors around the incubator. If there is a problem, an alarm sounds to alert the nurses.

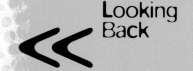

Looking Back

Babies on Display The first incubators were used in the late 19th century. At the Chicago World's Fair in 1933–34, premature babies in incubators were exhibited as an oddity that people lined up to see!

It took many years for incubators to come into common use in hospitals, but they now save many young lives

Kelly's Story

Kelly was born in the summer of 2003. She was tiny and in poor health because she had arrived three months early. Kelly lived in an incubator for many weeks, being helped with her breathing and treated with many different medicines.

At last, when Kelly was three months old, her parents were able to take her home. Today she is fine, but without the incubator, Kelly probably would have died.

Human Contact

We now know that it is very important for a baby to be touched and handled while it is in an incubator. Parents can stroke their babies and sometimes even hold them for a little while each day.

It may take days or weeks, but soon the baby should be strong enough to come out of the incubator and go home with its family.

Special instruments are being used by the doctor to help this baby start breathing.

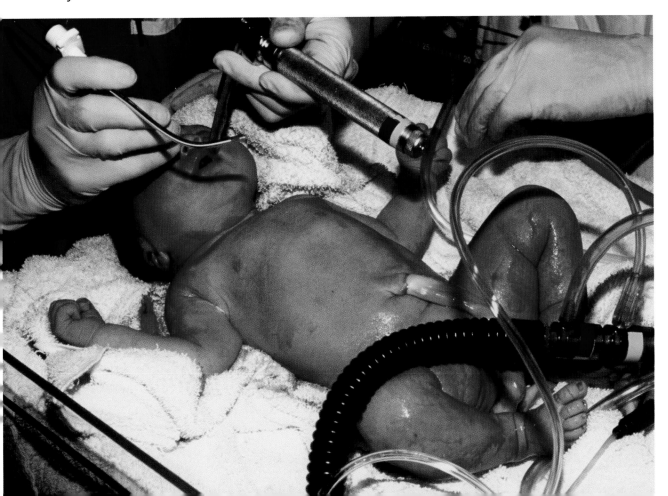

27

A laser is a device that makes a high-energy light beam. This beam of light can be used to cut human tissue like a tiny surgical knife. Laser beams are very narrow and can be precisely controlled. This is why they can be used to perform operations on delicate areas of the body.

Treating Cancer

Lasers are used today to operate on eyes, skin, feet, and sometimes even hearts. One very important use for lasers is in treating women who are at risk of cervical cancer. In this condition, some of the cells found in the cervix, or neck of the womb, show signs of becoming cancerous.

A laser can be used to destroy these cells before they do any harm. It does this without harming the normal cells in that area.

This woman is receiving laser eye treatment. Her head must be held still in a brace to ensure the laser reaches the right part of the eye.

Looking Back

From Factory to Hospital

First developed in 1964, lasers were used in factories where precision cutting was important. When lasers were first used in medicine around 20 years ago, doctors had to use adapted industrial lasers.

Today, modern medical lasers are designed specifically for use on human tissue. They have many special features that make them safer and more effective.

Laser Surgery for Eyes

Many people wear glasses or contact lenses to help them see. But some people now choose to have laser eye surgery instead. This type of surgery changes the shape of the cornea (the see-through covering at the front of the eye), which affects eyesight.

One of the most popular methods is called LASIK. It involves cutting a tiny flap in the cornea with a minute surgical tool, and then using a laser to cut away some of the corneal tissue underneath.

>> Looking Forward

Cosmetic Surgery It is likely that lasers will be used more and more in many areas of medicine. Cosmetic surgery, which involves changing the way a person looks, is one area that is starting to make use of lasers. Laser surgery is already being done to remove large birthmarks. It might also be able to make the skin look younger—which would be very popular with aging film and TV stars!

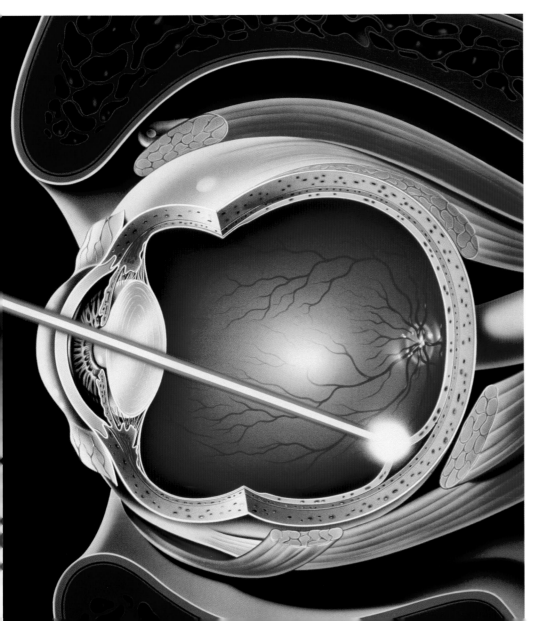

This cutaway picture of the back of the eye (the retina) shows where the beam of light goes during laser surgery.

420 B.C. Hippocrates begins the scientific study of medicine.

A.D. 1451 Nicholas of Cusa invents spectacles (glasses) for short-sightedness.

1628 William Harvey first describes the way blood circulates (goes around) the body.

1763 Claudius Aymand is the first to successfully remove the appendix.

1816 Rene Laennec invents the stethoscope.

1842 Crawford Long performs the first surgical operation using anesthesia (medicine to put the patient to sleep).

1859 Louis Pasteur suggests that some diseases may be caused by tiny living creatures (bacteria).

1867 Joseph Lister shows that using disinfectants during operations reduces the number of infections afterward.

1895 Wilhelm Roentgen discovers X rays.

1899 A new painkiller called aspirin is introduced.

1928 Alexander Fleming discovers penicillin, one of the first antibiotics (medicines that kill bacteria).

1933 Premature babies in incubators are displayed as an oddity at the Chicago World's Fair.

1943 The first artificial kidney is made by Willem Kolff.

1952 Paul Zoll develops one of the first artificial heart pacemakers.

1953 Surgeons perform the first successful open-heart surgery using a heart-lung machine at Jefferson Medical College in Philadelphia.

1953 James Watson and Francis Crick solved the puzzle of the structure of DNA, the chemical that carries genetic information.

1953 Jonas Salk successfully tests a new polio vaccine.

1954 The first successful human organ transplant is performed. A kidney taken from one identical twin is given to the other.

1957 Willem Kolff tests his artificial heart in animals.

1959 Wilson Greatbach keeps a patient alive for 18 months with his artificial pacemaker.

1964 Lasers are developed for use in industry.

1967 Christiaan Barnard performs the first successful heart transplant.

1973 Paul Christian Lauterbur publishes the first MRI (magnetic resonance imaging) body scan. This type of scanning soon becomes widely used.

1978 The first test-tube baby is born.

1982 Barney Clark survives 112 days with an artificial heart called the Jarvik 7.

1987 The first heart-lung transplant is performed.

1990 The Human Genome Project is launched. This is a study to find all the genes in the human body.

2000 The Human Genome Project delivers the first draft of the complete genetic information for the human body.

birthmark A harmless red or brown mark on the skin that is there at birth.

cancer A serious illness that often includes the growth of lumps (tumors) somewhere in the body.

carbon fiber A strong, light, man-made material.

cardiopulmonary bypass machine A machine that does the work of the heart and lungs (also called a heart-lung machine).

cervix The neck, or lower opening, of the womb (the female organ that holds a growing baby).

cochlea The snail-shaped organ that lies in the inner ear. It turns sound waves into electrical signals sent to the brain.

cornea The see-through part of the surface of the eyeball, which covers the colored iris and the black pupil.

defibrillator A machine that gives an electric shock to the heart to make it beat properly.

diagnosis The identification of a person's illness.

dialysis Using a machine to do the work of the kidneys. Dialysis machines get rid of unwanted liquid and chemicals in the blood.

donor Someone who gives a part of his or her body after death to help someone else.

donor card A card carried by people stating that they want to give a part of their body after death to help someone else.

echocardiogram An ultrasound scan of the heart.

endoscope A long, flexible tube with a camera at the end. It is used to look deep inside the body.

gallbladder A small organ in the stomach that makes a liquid needed to break down food.

hearing aid A small, electronic device that helps someone hear better.

heart-lung machine A machine that does the work of the heart and lungs (also called a cardiopulmonary bypass machine).

heart transplant When someone is given a new heart because his or her own doesn't work anymore.

implanted When a device is implanted, a surgeon cuts open the body, places the device inside, then sews the cut up.

incubator A special crib-like machine that is used to keep weak, newborn babies safe and warm.

intestine The long tube that food travels along inside the body.

iron lung A large ventilator that completely encloses a person from the neck down.

Kevlar A very strong, man-made material used in some artificial limbs and bullet-proof vests.

keyhole surgery Surgical operations performed through tiny cuts, with the surgeon using an endoscope to see what he or she is doing.

left ventricular assist device (LVAD) A small, electronic device that is implanted in the heart to help it do its work.

murmur An abnormal sound made by the heart. It can be heard with a stethoscope.

pacemaker Either the part of the heart that tells the rest of the heart muscle when to beat, or a man-made electronic device that does the same job.

paralyzed When people are paralyzed, they can no longer move a part of their body.

polio A serious illness caused by a virus. It can leave a person paralyzed (unable to move parts of his or her body).

premature A baby is premature if it is born weeks or months too early.

prosthesis Something artificial (man-made) that replaces a part of the body.

renal Having to do with the kidneys.

surgical wound A cut made in the skin by a surgeon while a person is asleep during an operation.

titanium A very strong, light metal.

ultrasound Sound waves that can be used to look inside the body.

urine The water passed out when a person goes to the bathroom.

vaccine A medicine or shot that is given to keep a person from getting an infection in the future.

ventilator A machine that pushes air into the lungs to help people who cannot breathe for themselves.

virtual Not real. A virtual image seems real but is actually made by a computer.

X rays Rays that can't be seen by our eyes but can be used to take pictures of the inside of the body.

Further Information

Further Reading

Action Pack: Human Body. New York: Dorling Kindersley Publishing, 2003.

Biesty, Stephen. *Incredible Body*. New York: Dorling Kindersley Publishing, 1998.

Hindley, Judy, and C. J. Rawson. *How Your Body Works*. Tulsa, Okla.: EDC Publishing, 1995.

Walker, Richard. *Genes and DNA*. Boston: Kingfisher Publications, 2003.

Web sites

http://www.howstuffworks.com
Covers several topics in medical technology, including X rays and various types of scanners.

http://www.bbc.co.uk/science/humanbody/
A Web site that looks at the human body and mind.

http://www.innerbody.com/
An exploration of the human anatomy, including animation, graphics, and descriptive links.

http://www.kidshealth.org/kid/body/mybody.html
Information and health tips for every part of the body.

http://yucky.kids.discovery.com/
A site full of gross, yucky, and cool facts about the body.

Index